budgerigar

understanding and
caring for your pet

Written by
Catherine Smith

©Toni McLellan –
www.toniwrites.com

budgerigar

understanding and
caring for your pet

Written by
Catherine Smith

Magnet & Steel Ltd

www.magnetsteel.com

All rights reserved. No part of this work may be reproduced, in any form or by any means, electronic or mechanical, including photocopying, recording or by any information storage and retrieval system, without the prior written permission of the publisher.

Copyright © Magnet & Steel Ltd 2014

Every reasonable care has been taken in the compilation of this publication. The Publisher and Author cannot accept liability for any loss, damage, injury or death resulting from the keeping of budgerigars by user(s) of this publication, from the use of any materials, equipment, methods or information recommended in this publication, from any errors or omissions that may be found in the text of this publication or that may occur at a future date, except as expressly provided by law.

No animals were harmed in the making of this book.

The 'he' pronoun is used throughout this book instead of the rather impersonal 'it', however no gender bias is intended.

Printed and bound in China.

ISBN: 978-1-907337-26-0
ISBN: 1-907337-26-1

Contents

Perfect pets   08

Special requirements   12

Where do budgerigars come from?   16

Becoming pets   20

What's in a name?   26

New developments   28

General appearance   32

Body language   40

Budgerigar colours   50

Important considerations   58

Sourcing a budgerigar   64

Budgerigar health check   68

Setting up home   72

Feeding budgerigars   82

Settling in   88

Establishing a routine   94

Preventative health care   100

Health problems   110

Common ailments   118

Weights & measures   128

Perfect pets

Perfect pets

Budgerigars, also known as parakeets, are the most popular of all the species of pet birds, and it is easy to see why:

• Budgerigars are small and so they do not need spacious accommodation. They can be housed in a cage and, as long as they have periods when they can exercise, they will not notice whether they are living in a high-rise apartment or in a country mansion.

• There are more than 100 different colours to choose from, so there are colours and markings to suit all tastes.

• With patience, budgerigars can become very tame and are easy to handle.

• They are social animals that enjoy company – both avian and human – but they can still be kept if you are out at work during the day.

• If you suffer from an allergy caused by animal fur, you may well find that you can live with a feathered friend.

However, it is important to check this out with your doctor before embarking on budgie ownership.

• Budgerigars have a good life expectancy of seven to eight years – and many live for longer. The world record for the oldest budgie goes to Charlie, who lived for an amazing 29 years and two months!

• Budgerigars are great pets for children. They are highly entertaining and will teach youngsters the responsibilities involved in caring for animals.

• They are also great pets for those getting on in years as they do not demand physical exertion in terms of needing to be exercised.

• Best of all, budgerigars are great communicators and you can form a real bond with your budgie. He may even learn to talk to you!

Special
requirements

Special requirements

Budgerigars are easy to care for, but like all animals they have their own special needs. If you take on a budgie, it is your responsibility to give him everything he needs. This includes:

• Providing a cage that is big enough for the number of birds you are keeping, and is equipped with suitable perches.

• Feeding the correct diet, which must include all the elements of nutrition which will keep your budgerigar healthy.

• Keeping the cage scrupulously clean. This will require daily attention and a thorough clean out once a week.

• Checking your budgie on a routine basis to ensure he is fit and healthy.

• Creating a budgie friendly environment so your budgie has time outside his cage where he can exercise safely.

• Giving your budgerigar companionship. A budgie will be miserable if he is kept on his own.

• Spending time with your budgie and handling him so he learns to enjoy human company.

Where do budgerigars come from?

The budgerigar is a member of hugely diverse and successful parrot family, which includes over 350 different species and can be found in Africa, Asia, North and South America and Australia.

Parrots are also known as psittacines, and they are divided into three main groups:

• Psittacidae: the true parrots, which includes the largest number of species, including budgerigars/parakeets.

• Cacatuidae: all species of cockatoo.

• Strigopidae: New Zealand parrots.

Budgerigars come from central Australia and in their native land they live in huge flocks, numbering tens of thousands of birds, flying over the hot, dry grasslands. They make a spectacular sight – but you will not see the dazzling array of colours that we are familiar with in pet budgies. Wild budgerigars are all the same colour – they are green with yellow faces and have black markings on their wings. They are smaller and thinner than pet budgerigars.

In the wild, budgerigars live on grasses, grass seeds eucalyptus leaves, berries and, sometimes, insects. In the hot, dry conditions, food and water is often scarce, so budgerigars are constantly on the move, searching for fresh supplies. Activity begins at dawn when the flock goes out to feed. During the middle of the day the birds rest, finding what shade they can among the sparse foliage of the trees, before going out to feed again until dusk.

Budgerigars must watch out for hawks which will hunt them on the wing, and for snakes, which will attack them when they are on the ground. However, the greatest peril they face is drought. Adults birds will die if they cannot get sufficient fresh water to drink, and chicks, which are particularly vulnerable, will die in their nests.

When the rain comes, budgerigars will suspend their nomadic existence and settle down to breed. The rainfall ensures a plentiful supply of food for the flock which will, in turn, give the growing chicks their best chance of survival.

Adult birds build their nests in the hollows of trees and, like most members of the parrot family, a male and female will form a strong pair bond, and will raise their chicks together. As the adults breed en masse, the chicks in a flock will all be roughly the same age. This means they will all be ready to take their place in the flock when it is time to move on.

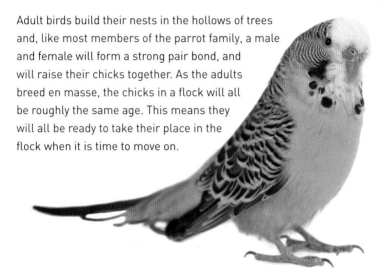

Becoming
pets

Becoming pets

How did the budgerigar, a small, native bird from Australia, become the most popular pet bird, finding its way into millions of homes across the world?

The story begins in 1768 when Captain James Cook, an English explorer, set off in the Endeavour on a voyage to the South Pacific. He first reached Tahiti and then sailed on to New Zealand, where he took possession of the two main islands and charted 3860 km of coastline. In 1770 he reached the east coast of Australia and claimed the territory for Great Britain, calling it New South Wales.

The sailors who travelled with him came back to England telling tales of the beautiful green birds that flew in such large flocks that they blotted out the sun. They said that when the birds landed on the branches of a dead tree, it was as if the tree had come back to life.

But it was not until 1840 that the first budgerigars arrived in England when a pair was brought back from Australia by the naturalist and explorer, John Gould. These small, green birds, measuring about 10cm (4in) attracted the interest of breeders who tried keeping them in captivity, mostly in zoos.

They had heard that budgerigars nested in the hollows of trees and discovered that a coconut shell, with holes drilled into it, was readily accepted as a nest. Budgerigars thrived in their new environment and were soon breeding in large numbers.

What's in a name?

The budgerigar's scientific name is Melopsittacus Undulates. Its common name the budgerigar – or budgie – dates back to its Australian roots.

When early English settlers arrived in Australia they asked native Aborigines, in sign language, the name of the little green bird that flew in such large flocks. The reply was "betchery-gah", and the settlers adopted the name 'budgerigar'. Many years later, when a linguist translated the Aboriginal language, it was discovered that "betchery-gah" meant "good to eat"!

In the USA, the budgerigar has always been known as a parakeet, often shortened to 'keet'. In fact, the name parakeet is used for many species of parrot with long tail feathers, but it has been universally adopted for the small Australian species, which has become the number one pet bird.

New developments

Similar developments in breeding budgerigars were underway in Europe but, in 1870, news broke that caused a sensation among the new budgerigar breeding fraternity. In Belgium, a pure yellow bird was born. It had red eyes and no black markings. The owner thought he would make a fortune breeding this brand new variety – but the bird turned out to be a one-off. It was some years before a new colour appeared; it was yellow with pale markings on its wings and had black eyes.

There was clearly the potential to develop new varieties, but, to begin with, progress was slow. A blue budgerigar, with black markings and a pure white face, appeared at the beginning of the 20th century, and in 1910 sky-blue birds were exhibited at a show in the Horticultural Hall in London.

Japanese royalty became intrigued by these beautiful blue birds, and it was rumoured that they paid a huge sum to import a pair of birds to set up their own breeding programme. It then became the fashion among Japanese nobility to give blue budgerigars as love tokens, and so their numbers, and their popularity grew.

New colours or 'mutations' appeared – more yellows, now known as lutinos, all-white albinos, birds with coloured patches known as pieds. As the hobby of breeding budgerigars grew, so did the varieties and now there are over 100 to choose from.

At first, it was only the wealthy who could afford to keep budgerigars – the first breed club in the UK, the Budgerigar Society, had King George V as its patron. But as they became more common, they became more affordable. When Europeans emigrated to the USA in the early part of the 20th century, they took their favourite pet birds with them, and so the budgie or 'keet' arrived in America.

The budgerigar's world

In order to keep a budgerigar as a pet, it is important to understand how his body functions and how he sees the world.

General appearance

General appearance

The budgerigar is a small, long-tailed bird, measuring 18cm (7in) from head to tail, although some of the more exotic varieties may be 25cm (10in) in length. The budgie's body, is covered in short, contour feathers, and is streamlined, which is essential for flight.

Beak

The beak is a vital piece of equipment which has a variety of uses. Its primary use is for cracking open seeds, but it is also used for preening, climbing and for investigating. It is composed of keratin, which is the same substance found in our fingernails. The beak grows continually; it is estimated that a budgerigar's beak will grow 7.5cm (3in) in a year. However, continual use will mean that that it will wear down naturally. If the beak grows too long, there is likely to be a fault in conformation, and veterinary advice should be sought.

©Toni McLellan –
www.toniwrites.com

Eyes

The budgerigar has three eyelids to protect its eyes. As well as an upper and lower eyelid, there is a third eyelid which covers the surface of the eyeball. Budgerigars have different eye colours, depending on their overall colouring, and because of the way the eyes are placed, a budgie can see to the side as well as in front.

Nostrils

A budgerigar's nostrils are located at the junction between the head and the beak. There is a small area of fleshy skin, above the nostrils, which is known as the cere. Male budgies (cocks) have blue ceres; females (hens) have brown ceres.

Ears

These are positioned on either side of the head, but they are hard to see as they are hidden beneath feathers. If your budgie has a bath, you may see two small ear holes. Compared to people, budgerigars have poor hearing.

©Toni McLellan –
www.toniwrites.com

Wings

The wings have long flight feathers which create a wide wingspan, essential for flying.

Tail

This has long feathers, which help the bird to balance during flight.

Rump

On the lower back, the budgerigar has a gland which secretes an oily substance used to keep the feathers in good order. You will see a budgerigar going to this gland and then spreading the oil over his feathers when he is preening.

Toes

A budgerigar has two sets of toes – one pair point forward and the other pair point backwards. They are used for perching, climbing and investigating.

Vent

Situated under the tail, this is an opening which is used for breeding and for getting rid of waste.

Body language

Like all animals, a budgerigar conveys his feeling through his body language. It's just a matter of knowing what to look for!

You will see some of the body language on a daily basis, as part of your budgie's normal behaviour. But some is more rarely seen and is a response to a specific situation.

Standing on one foot

This is a budgerigar's normal resting position.

Beak tucked under back feathers

Most budgerigars adopt this position when they are sleeping.

Rubbing the beak on the perch

This is a way of cleaning the beak, usually seen after a budgerigar has finished eating.

Yawning

A budgerigar will yawn exactly as we do. However, if you see a budgie yawning repeatedly, he may be suffering from a shortage of oxygen and you will need to seek expert help.

Stretching legs backwards

This is the budgerigar's version of stretching and he will often do this after a period of rest.

Lifting the wings sideways

This is generally a form of stretching, but a male may do it to intimidate another bird by trying to look bigger, or if he is trying to impress a female.

Raised wings

You may see your budgerigar on his perch with his wings raised if he is hot and is trying to cool down. It can also be a sign of distress if he is panting with an open beak and closing his eyes for brief periods.

Preening another bird

This is a way of cementing a bond and is seen between male and female, and also among close companions of the same sex.

Shaking the feathers

This is a way of getting rid of dirt and other particles that have been loosened when the bird is preening. But it can also indicate a change of mood.

Scratching

A budgerigar will use his beak to preen his feathers and relieve itchiness. Sometimes there may be an awkward place and you will see the bird rub his body against a perch.

Puffing up the feathers

A budgerigar will do this when he feels cold. It is a way of trapping air between the feathers, which will form a layer of insulation. He may also puff his feathers when he is happy and contented, or when he is excited. A male may show off by puffing up his head feathers and displaying his tail feathers.

Flattening the feathers

Hopefully, you will not see this as it is a sign of fear.

Regurgitating

You may see a budgerigar regurgitating seed and feeding it to another bird. This is normal behaviour between breeding birds; a cock will feed a hen in this way when she is incubating eggs, and a hen will regurgitate seeds for her chicks. Companion budgies will regurgitate seeds for each other, and you may see a budgie regurgitate when he is perched in front of a mirror to feed his own reflection!

Verbal communication

Budgerigars are great communicators and you will soon know what mood your budgie is in by the sound he is making. Budgerigars will chirrup, chatter and warble to themselves in a low key as a sign of contentment, and males have a singing repertoire which is used to impress females. They are great mimics, and will readily copy different sounds which could include the calls of other birds, the vacuum cleaner, the telephone, as well as human voices.

Puck, a budgerigar who lived in California, USA, knew a record-breaking 1,728 words when he died in 1994. Most pet budgies will not rival this – but with time and patience, most budgies will learn to say a few words or phrases.

A female may learn to talk, but a male is capable of making a wider range of sounds, and will instinctively want to improve his repertoire.

There are some other sounds to listen out for:

Look at this!

Budgerigars are inquisitive birds, and if you hear a cry of "backpack ack", often accompanied by bobbing, it means your budgie has discovered something new.

Beak grinding

You will have to listen carefully to hear this. A budgerigar may grind his beak very quietly when he is resting, or just before he goes to sleep. It is a sign that the bird is relaxed and content.

Distress call

If your budgerigar is stressed and unhappy, he will show it in his body language (see Raised Wings, page 42), and may call out "fweep" in a high-pitched voice.

Alarm call

This is a sharp, hissed "tsst tsst" sound which budgerigars use to communicate possible danger. On hearing it, a budgerigar will usually take flight.

Screeeching

This is a cry of alarm or fear, and the budgerigar will be tense, with feathers flattened, ready to take off.

Budgerigar colours

The budgerigar has come a long way from the small, plain green and yellow bird that flew in vast flocks across the grasslands of central Australia. Not only is it already available in a stunning range of colours and markings, but breeders are working on new varieties all the time.

There are many serious avian enthusiasts who show their birds and compete for the top honours. The sport is highly competitive and judges look for birds that come closest to perfection in terms of colour, markings, plumage and general conformation.

Pet owners have their favourite colours, but most of us will not aspire to own the rare, exotic varieties that are produced by specialist breeders. However, it is interesting to have a look at the range of colours that are available.

The basic colours for budgerigars are blue and green, but each of these colours comes in three shades.

Blue budgerigars may be:

• Sky blue: The lightest shade.

• Cobalt blue: The middle shade.

• Mauve: The darkest shade.

In each of these colours, the face is white, the body is a solid colour and the wings have black bars.

Green budgerigars may be:

• Light green: The lightest shade.

• Dark green: The middle shade.

• Olive green: The darkest shade.

In each of these colours, the face is yellow. As with the blue variety, the body is a solid colour and the wings have black bars.

Adding colours

Grey

The colour grey can be added to all six varieties and has a different effect on each one. In green budgies, the colour becomes varying shades of khaki, whereas in the blue series, the budgie may be light, mid or dark grey.

Cinnamon

The addition of cinnamon creates more delicate shades in the six blue/green varieties and the bars on the wings are brown.

Opaline

This has the effect of softening the body colour so that it is paler, and the barring on the head and shoulders is greatly reduced. The body colour is more pronounced on the wings, which sets off the black barring.

Subtracting colours

A budgerigar can be bred without colour pigment. In the green varieties, this produces a lutino – an all-yellow bird with red eyes; in blue varieties it produces an albino – an all-white bird with red eyes.

Pied varieties

These are the most colourful budgerigars and are especially popular with pet owners as no two pieds are the same. There are different types of pied budgerigars:

Dominant pied

In the green shades, the body colour is solid green with irregular patches of yellow. The wings have patches of yellow, the eyes are black with a white iris and the feet are mottled pink. In the blue varieties, the body has irregular white patches, and white patches on the wings.

Recessive pieds

In the green shades, the body has bright grass green and yellow patches and the wings are mainly yellow with irregular black bars. The eyes are black. In the blue varieties, the patches on the body are bright azure blue and white.

Other varieties

Yellow-faced

The yellow-faced budgerigar only appears in the blue series. This bird has a yellow face and head and is also available in the pied variety, which makes it the most colourful of all budgerigars.

Clearwings

These beautiful birds have, as their name suggests, clear wings – pure white in the blue varieties, and pure yellow in the green varieties.

Spangled

This applies to all the colours. The wings are the same colour as the body, with small black marks on the tips.

Crested/tufted

This variety is marked by different plumage on the head. A crested budgerigar has a fringe of feathers all round his head; the tufted variety has a crest which sticks up at the front of his head. This variation applies to all colours – but it can be quite difficult to find.

Important considerations

Now you have decided that budgerigars are the pets for you, there are some important decisions to make before you buy.

Colour

As we have seen, there are lots to choose from – and it all comes down to personal preference. Obviously, the more exotic varieties will be more expensive and you will need to go to a specialist breeder.

Male or female?

You may need an expert to help you distinguish between males and females – particularly when the birds are young. A young hen will have a blue-white cere (the waxy skin above the nostrils), which will become brown with age. A young cock has a pinkish-purple cere which will turn blue.

All budgerigars are individuals and you will not see a great difference in temperament between males and females – particularly if they are not being used for breeding. However, if you want to teach your budgerigar to talk, you may find that a cock is a more willing pupil.

What age?

Ideally, you should buy a budgerigar that is between two and three months of age. By this time, the bird is fully independent, but is young enough to tame and to form a close bond with his human family.

If you go to a breeder, you will be able to find out the age of the budgerigar you are buying. It will also be fitted with a ring around its leg which has a personal ID number as well as the year the budgerigar was born.

If you are buying from another source, you can check the age by looking at the plumage. A young bird has his first moult at three to four months of age. Until then, he will have black bars on his head reaching down to the cere. After moulting, the black bars disappear. However, this does not apply to lutino, albino or recessive pied varieties.

Another clue is to look at the throat spots, which are dark spots at the front of the throat. In adult birds, these will be large and distinct, whereas in young birds they will be small spots or flecks. Again, this does not apply to lutinos or albinos.

More than one?

As we have discovered, budgerigars are sociable birds and will not thrive if they are kept on their own. Unless you plan to get involved in breeding, the best plan is to go for same sex pairs – two cocks or two hens. They may not form the close bond seen in breeding birds, but they will soon become very good friends.

Cage or aviary?

There are two ways of keeping budgerigars – in a cage inside your home or in an outside aviary. Budgerigars are adaptable birds and will thrive in both environments as long as they are well cared for.

Budgerigar breeders, who have lots of birds, will generally opt for an aviary. This will usually have a large outside flight area, which is fenced with wire netting, and an inside sleeping compartment.

There is no doubt that budgies enjoy the freedom to fly in an aviary, and the company of other birds. However, if you keep your budgerigars in a cage, they will be perfectly content as long as the cage is spacious, and they have opportunities for free flying exercise.

Sourcing a budgerigar

It is vitally important to get off to a good start and buy a healthy budgerigar from a reputable source. There are three options:

Specialist breeder

This is the best place to go if you want a specific colour or variety, or if you have plans to show your budgerigars in competition. A specialist breeder will be striving to produce birds that most closely match the breed standard, and will also be able to give you invaluable help and advice when it comes to breeding.

Pet store

This is a good source, as long as you go to a reputable pet store that has knowledgeable staff who can help you make your choice.

Rescue centres

There are specialist budgerigar rescue centres and all-breed parrot rescue centres that find homes for birds that are no longer wanted by their original owners. Unfortunately, the budgerigar, which is often bought as a children's pet, can find himself homeless through no fault of his own if children lose interest.

You are doing a great service if you can offer an older budgerigar a home, but you need to bear in mind that he may not be as tame as a bird that you have had from an early age.

Budgerigar health check

Budgerigar health check

When you go to buy a budgerigar, check out the following to ensure your bird is fit and healthy:

• Inspect the living conditions. They should be clean and hygienic, with no evidence of stale odour. They should be sufficiently spacious for the number of birds that are accommodated.

• The budgerigars should be alert and inquisitive, showing no signs of stress.

• The birds should be standing on their perches with ease, showing no signs of discomfort.

• The eyes should be bright and clear.

• The plumage should be sleek.

• Breathing is rapid in a healthy bird, but it should be quiet.

• The vent, which is the opening from which waste is excreted, should be clean.

Setting up home

Setting up home

When you are buying a cage for your budgerigars, the golden rule is: the bigger the better. Obviously this will depend on how many birds you are keeping, and what you can afford. But it is important to remember that the cage is your budgerigar's home and he will spend a considerable amount of time in there. Therefore, the more spacious it is, the happier he will be.

Many first-time owners make the mistake of thinking that a tall, cylindrical cage will make a good home. But this is not the case. A budgerigar does not fly up and down; he flies from side to side, alighting on different perches. Therefore he will appreciate a cage that is as wide as possible.

If you are planning to keep two birds (or a maximum of four), the minimum size is 51cm x 36cm x 36cm (20in x 14in x 14in).

Locating the cage

Budgerigars are hardy birds – but there are two things they hate – cold draughts and direct sunlight. When you are planning where to site your cage, it is essential to bear this in mind.

To escape draughts, the cage should be at least 1.5 metres (5 feet) from the ground, and should not be near a window. Budgerigars do not tolerate extremes of heat, so avoid a room such as conservatory, which can be very warm in the day and cold at night. Your budgerigars will enjoy being in a busy room where there is plenty of activity, but if you have an open fire, the cage will have to be located elsewhere as budgerigars cannot cope with smoke in the atmosphere. For the same reason, you must avoid siting your birds in the kitchen.

Furnishings

Once you have your cage in situ, you will need to equip it for your budgerigars.

Landing platform

This fits on to the doorway of the cage, and allows your budgerigar to fly back into his cage after free-flying exercise.

Perches

Your budgerigars will need a variety of perches, at different levels and of varying width. If you watch a budgie land on a perch, you will see how he uses his feet to balance and hold on. If the perches are identical, he will use the same part of his feet every time, and they will soon become sore and uncomfortable.

Floor covering

The best type to use is ready-made sand sheets which can be changed easily. Budgerigars like the rough surface which they can scratch, keeping their nails in trim.

Water bottle

Your budgerigars will need a ready supply of fresh water. This can be supplied by fixing a water bottle to the side of the cage.

Bowls

You will need two bowls: one for seed and one for grit (see page 85) Those made of ceramic are easy to clean and will not get tipped over. Make sure you do not place them underneath perches as the contents will be spoiled by droppings.

Toys

Budgerigars are clever little birds and they are stimulated by a variety of different toys. Do not make the mistake of cramming the cage with toys so your budgies have no room to move! It is far better to rotate toys on a daily basis to provide something new to play with.

Bear in mind that budgerigars have sharp beaks and like to peck at their toys. For this reason it is better to avoid those made of plastic and opt for robust, wooden toys instead.

Budgerigars will enjoy the following:

• Ladder: Your budgie will love climbing up and down a ladder, but make sure there is sufficient space between the rungs so he does not get stuck.

• Mirror: Your budgie will sing to his reflection as though it were another bird.

• Swing: Perfect for a budgie to practise his acrobatic skills.

• Bell: You may get fed up with this before your budgie does!

Indoor flight

If possible, you should provide an enclosed area where your budgerigars can fly in safety. You can buy an indoor flight which has the advantage that it can be stored when it is not in use. Many owners allow their budgerigars to fly freely in a room, but be careful to ensure that doors and windows are closed.

Feeding budgerigars

In order for a budgerigar to be fit and healthy, he must be fed a diet that will meet all his nutritional requirements. Fortunately, budgerigars are not fussy feeders so you should have no difficulty in providing a well balanced diet, along with a few tasty treats.

Seed mix

Seeds are the main component of a budgerigar's diet – and there are a number of seed mixes which have been designed especially for them. The best type to buy is a mix that contains red rape, linseed or niger as well canary and millet seeds.

A budgie breaks open a seed with his beak to get at the inner part, which is known as the kernel. The outer part – the husk – is discarded, and you will need to clear these leftovers on a daily basis, otherwise the new seeds will be buried in old husks.

Seed diets are also available in pellet from, specially formulated to meet a budgerigar's nutritional needs.

Grit

This is not food – but it is an essential aid to digestion, and should be provided in a bowl, alongside the seed mix. A budgerigar swallows seeds whole, and they pass into the gizzard. This is like a grinding machine which will break down the seeds, but it needs grit in order to function.

Green food

A variety of greens, including grass that is going to seed, dandelion leaves, chickweed and salad greens, will add variety to your budgerigar's diet, but they should be provided only in small quantities. If you are picking leaves from your garden make sure they have not been sprayed with toxic chemicals.

You can a buy a pot of seeds from a pet store; when you start watering, the seeds will start to sprout, providing an ultra fresh snack for your budgies.

Minerals

A budgerigar needs the correct balance of minerals in his diet, and these are most easily provided by a mineral block which also contains iodine. A cuttlefish bone, attached to the bars of the cage, is an excellent source of calcium.

Treats

Budgerigars love millet, and will greatly appreciate a millet spray attached to the bars of the cage. However, millet is fattening, and should only be provided as an occasional treat. Your budgie will also enjoy healthy snacks, such as slices of apple and carrot. These are very useful when you are hand training your budgerigar.

Settling in

Arriving in a new home is a daunting experience, so give your budgerigar a chance to settle in his cage before trying to handle him.

If you are introducing a second budgie, you should keep the birds in separate cages for the first couple of weeks, but within sight of each other. This gives the birds a chance to get to know each other in safety, and it also eliminates the risk of spreading disease. When your new bird has settled, and you are confident that he is fit and healthy, you can move the two birds in together.

The key to taming a budgerigar is to take things very slowly:

• To start with, talk to your budgie every time you are near his cage so that he gets used to the sound of your voice.

• When you change the seed bowl, be slow and steady in your movements so he gets used to your hand and does not see it as a threat.

• When you are sure your budgie is relaxed and happy in his cage, you can start finger-training him. First get a piece of millet spray, then open the cage door and put your hand, holding the millet, inside the cage.

• Position your hand close to where your budgie is perching and hold it very still. Eventually, the budgie will hop on to your hand to nibble the millet. Practise this over a period of days to allow your budgie to grow in confidence.

• When your budgerigar has accepted your hand as a
perch, hold out your finger and see if he will hop on.
Wait until your budgie readily accepts your finger as
a perch before you let him out of the cage.

Free flying exercise

All budgerigars benefit from free flying – it exercises their bodies and stimulates their minds. Before your budgie is allowed out of cage, check the following:

• All doors and windows are closed. Curtains should be drawn to prevent the budgie flying into glass. Mirrors should also be covered.

• Other pets should be taken out of the room, and all members of the household should be aware that your budgie is out of his cage.

• Potential hazards for free-flying budgerigars include electric fans, lighted candles, poisonous household plants, standing water, such as a fish tank, and open fires. Make sure all these dangers are eliminated before you allow your budgies to fly.

When your budgerigar has had sufficient exercise, ask him to hop back on to your finger and then you can transfer him to the safety of his cage.

Establishing a routine

When you are caring for a budgerigar, you are looking after the bird himself, but you are also responsible for his living conditions, which must be monitored on a daily basis and kept scrupulously clean.

Daily tasks

Get into the habit of checking your budgerigars every day to ensure they are in good health.

You should also:

• Clear away the empty husks from the seed bowl and replenish if necessary.

• Check the water bottle and refill if needed.

• Remove the sandpaper at the bottom of the cage and replace with a new sheet.

• Remove greens if they are wilting.

• Replace one of the toys in the cage with something new for your budgies to play with.

• If you are using an indoor flight, clean up droppings.

Weekly tasks

You will need to move your budgerigars to a safe place when you do the weekly clean out. You may have a second cage or you can put them in their indoor flight, if you have one, to give the opportunity for free-flying exercise while you work.

• Take everything out of the cage, including the floor covering so you can give it a thorough clean.

• Fixtures, such as perches, must also be wiped down carefully.

• Food bowls and toys should all be washed before replacing them.

Hot water tends to kill most bacteria, but you can also buy specially manufactured cleaners and sprays from pet stores which are safe to use.

Preventative
health care

A problem spotted early – or prevented – can stop serious health issues arising. It is also important to ensure that your budgerigars are well, happy and comfortable.

Beak

The beak grows throughout a budgerigar's life but, again, it should wear down naturally. Problems will usually only occur if the beak is misaligned in some way. If you notice that your budgie is having difficulty feeding – struggling to extract the kernel from the husk – he probably has a problem with his beak. In this instance, it is best to ask the vet or an experienced bird-keeper to trim the beak for you. It is essential that the correct shape is maintained and so it is a job for the expert.

Nails

If your budgerigar has a rough surface to scratch on, and has a variety of different perches, his nails should wear down naturally. However, you need to check that they do not become overgrown as this will result in difficulty in perching. This may apply particularly to an older bird that is less active.

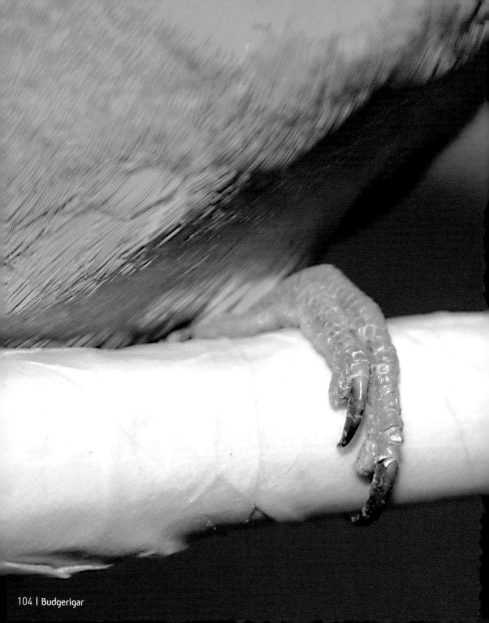

Claws can be clipped with guillotine style nail-clippers. It is a relatively simple procedure, but if you are concerned, asked an experienced bird-keeper or your vet to do the job for you.

The aim is to cut the tip of the nail, avoiding the blood vessels. If this is done correctly, it is not painful for the budgerigar, and if the bird is held in a firm grasp, he should not struggle unduly.

Preening and moulting

A budgerigar will keep his feathers in good order by preening. He uses his beak as a grooming tool to remove dirt and other particles, and covers the feathers with an oily, water-resistant substance which he secretes from a gland in his rump. Budgies will preen each other, helping to reach the more awkward places, and you will find that your budgie loves to have the top of his head scratched – a place he cannot reach. You may find your budgie returns the compliment and will preen your hair and eyebrows!

In order to preen himself properly, a budgerigar needs access to water. You can provide a saucer of lukewarm water in the cage and watch him take a bath, or if your budgie is very tame, he will enjoy being gently sprayed with water. You can use the type of bottle that is used for plants.

A budgerigar will moult several times a year. The main moult is usually in the autumn, and you will find tiny contour feathers from the body in the bottom of the cage. The flight feathers on the wings and the tail feathers will also be shed and will gradually regrow. At this time, budgerigars are very susceptible to draughts, so check the siting of the cage and place a light cover over it, if necessary.

Egg laying

If you own a hen budgie, you may find that she lays an egg, even though she does not have a male partner. Obviously, the egg is unfertilised, and although egg laying in this way is not harmful, it can deplete the hen's calcium supplies.

If you see an egg in the cage, do not remove it, as you will encourage the hen to lay more. Simply replace it in the cage after cleaning. It is only if the egg gets broken that it needs to be removed.

After two or three weeks, the egg laying cycle will be over and you can remove eggs from the cage. The problem is unlikely to arise again for a considerable amount of time.

©Jen
www.puppiesareprozac.com

Health problems

Health
problems

We are fortunate that the budgerigar is a hardy bird, bred to survive in tough conditions in the wilds of Australia. Our pet budgerigars maybe a little more pampered, but essentially this is a bird without exaggeration and as a result suffers from relatively few serious health problems.

Signs of a sick bird

You will know if your budgerigar is unwell if you see any of the following signs of ill health:

Loss of appetite

It is sometimes hard to know exactly how much your budgerigars are eating, but if you check leftovers on a daily basis you should get a reasonably good idea of what is 'normal' for your budgies. If food is ignored, or your budgerigar seems to have problems with feeding, it is a cause for concern.

Droppings

The excreta produced by budgerigars is a good indicator of their health status. You need to look for changes in colour, volume and consistency. Droppings should be dark and firm with a white urine portion in the middle. If they are very wet and loose, your budgerigar is suffering from some form of digestive upset. This may be caused by what you have been feeding – too much green food, perhaps – but if the problem continues for more than a day you should seek veterinary advice. If you see undigested food in the droppings, you should call in expert help without delay.

Breathing

Signs of laboured or noisy breathing, accompanied by clicking or gasping, is a sign of respiratory problems. Your budgerigar will appear distressed and you need to seek help urgently.

Plumage

A budgerigar in good health has sleek plumage, which lies close to his body. When he is moulting, he may look a little untidy, but you should be concerned if you see any signs of balding or abnormal feather growth. Incorrect diet or lack of sunlight can be the cause of this problem, but you will need an expert to make a diagnosis.

©Toni McLellan –
www.toniwrites.com

E R

Fluffed feathers

A budgerigar will fluff out his feathers when he is cold so you may need to move the cage to a warmer location. Budgerigars can fluff out their feathers when they are happy and relaxed, but a bird that is cold will generally have a hunched body posture and will appear dejected.

Abnormal beak

If the beak is misaligned, it may not wear down naturally which will cause considerable discomfort. The first indication will be problems with feeding. You should also look out for changes in the beak's colour or texture, as this can be the result of a dietary imbalance which would need to be remedied.

Lethargy

As you get to know your budgerigar, you will tune in to his personality and know what is normal behaviour for him. If your budgie is acting out of character – particularly if he seems listless and lethargic – it could be an indication that he is feeling unwell. Monitor him closely for a couple of days, and if there is no improvement, seek expert help.

Discharge from nostrils/sneezing

The nostrils should be free from discharge. A clear discharge could indicate a sinus irritation caused by dust or pollen. It is more serious if you see a yellow or green-coloured discharge. In this situation, you should seek veterinary advice without delay.

Budgerigars cannot withstand ill health for long periods and tend to deteriorate quickly. So, if you see signs of ill health in your budgerigars, seek veterinary advice immediately.

Common ailments

Common ailments

There are a number of ailments that can affect budgerigars. Early diagnosis and treatment are most likely to lead to a successful outcome.

Scaly face

This condition is also known as scaly beak and scaly leg. It is caused by a mite, Cnemidocoptes pilae, which is transmitted from bird to bird by direct contact. The mite burrows under the horny upper layer of skin and causes crusting and scaling. Treatment involves painting a pesticidal preparation on to the affected areas.

Inflamed eyes

If a budgerigar gets something in his eye, such as
seed husk, he may scratch it, or rub his eye on the
perch in an attempt to relieve the irritation. In fact,
this usually causes the eye to become sore and
inflamed. You can try wiping the eye with cotton wool
soaked in diluted eye lotion (50 per cent eye lotion
to 50 per cent water). If this does not
help, consult a vet who will be able
to prescribe ointment.

Bumble foot

This is when a bird has an infected foot, which may become tender and inflamed. It is often caused by perches that are the wrong diameter, as the bird continually puts pressure on one part of his foot. Treatment is with antibiotics.

Respiratory infections

Members of the parrot family, including budgerigars, can be prone to respiratory infections. The most common signs are laboured breathing and a bubbly discharge from the nostrils. Antibiotics need to be administered without delay.

Growths

Fatty growths on the abdomen, and internal growths which may cause lameness by pressing down on nerves to the leg, are not uncommon in budgerigars. A cyst, resulting from bacterial infection, can be treated with antibiotics. Tumours of the uropygial gland, which secretes the oils that are used for preening, may respond to surgical intervention.

Egg binding

If a non-breeding hen lays an infertile egg, she will suffer no ill effects. However, occasionally the egg becomes stuck and you may see the hen straining as she tries to pass it. It may be partially visible inside the cloaca. Veterinary intervention is generally required, and sometimes surgery will be needed.

Digestive disorders

The first sign of this will usually be loose or discoloured droppings. A change to a plain seed diet may solve the problem, but if there is an infection, treatment will be needed. This can be given in the form of antibiotic seed, and a probiotic can be added to drinking water to restore the normal, healthy bacteria in the gut.

Goitre

This is an inflammation of the thyroid glands, which are situated in the neck. As the glands enlarge, the bird may suffer loss of voice and may have difficulty breathing. The cause is lack of iodine which can be rectified by supplementing the diet or adding iodine to the drinking water.

Feather loss

If your budgerigar suffers loss of feathers at times other than when he is moulting, you will need to investigate as there are a number of possible causes. It could be the result of mites or lice, and there is also a condition known as French Moult, which causes the feathers to grow abnormally.

You must also ensure that your budgerigar is not feather plucking out of boredom. This used to be relatively common – particularly when budgies were kept on their own. If you suspect this may be the reason, try providing more mental stimulation, or increase free flying opportunities, so your budgerigar has more to occupy his mind.

Summing up

The budgerigar is the perfect pet to keep in so many ways – beautiful to look at, alert, intelligent and entertaining – he really does have it all. Make sure you keep your half of the bargain and provide the essential care and companionship your budgerigar needs in order to live a long, happy, healthy and fulfilled life.

Weights & measures

If you prefer your units in pounds and inches, you can use this conversion chart:

Length in inches	Length in cm	Weight in kg	Weight in lbs
1	2.5	0.5	1.1
2	5.1	0.7	1.5
3	7.6	1	2.2
4	10.2	1.5	3.3
5	12.7	2	4.4
8	20.3	3	6.6
10	25.4	4	8.8
15	38.1	5	11

Measurements rounded to 1 decimal place.